My War
EVACUEE

Peter Hepplewhite

H O D D E R
Wayland

an imprint of Hodder Children's Books

Produced for Hodder Wayland by
Discovery Books Ltd
Unit 3, 37 Watling Street, Leintwardine, Shropshire SY7 0LW

First published in 2003 by Hodder Wayland, an imprint of Hodder Children's Books

British Library Cataloguing in Publication Data
Hepplewhite, Peter
    Evacuee. - (My war)
    1.World War, 1939-1945 - Evacuation of civilians - Great
    Britain - Juvenile literature 2.World War, 1939-1945 -
    Children - Great Britain - Juvenile Literature 3.Great
    Britain - George VI, 1936-1952 - Juvenile literature
    I. Title II. Williams, Gianna
    940.5'3161'0941

ISBN 0 7502 4219 1

Printed and bound in Hong Kong

Series editor: Gianna Williams
Designer: Ian Winton
Picture research: Rachel Tisdale

Hodder Children's Books would like to thank the following for the loan of their material:
Beamish Museum: pp. 13 (top), 27; Hulton Archive: *cover* (children on farm), pp. 8, 10, 12, 16 (bottom),
18 (bottom), 19, 22, 23; Hulton-Deutsch Collection/Corbis: pp. 13 (bottom), 14, 15 (bottom), 21; Imperial
War Museum: *cover* (train), pp. 7, 9 11, 26, 29 (top); Peter Hepplewhite: p. 6; Public Records Office: p. 7;
Robert Opie Collection: pp.15 (top), 16 (top), 18 (top), 20 (top).

The publishers would also like to thank John Campbell, Eileen Salter, Agnes Conway, Alan Reid,
Ken MacMillan Studios and the Evacuees Reunion Association
for their assistance and the loan of their material.

Hodder Children's Books
A division of Hodder Headline Limited
338 Euston Road
London NW1 3BH

Contents

Evacuees

On 3 September 1939, Britain went to war against Germany – the Second World War (1939-1945) had begun. Everyone expected British towns and cities to be attacked by German bombers and thousands of people to die.

JOHN CAMPBELL

John was born in Glasgow in 1934. His father worked as a boiler-maker for the local gas company. His family lived in Scotstoun, near the River Clyde and the shipyards. John was evacuated from Glasgow to Lanark in the Upper Clyde valley in 1941.

EILEEN SALTER

Eileen was born in 1926. She lived in Catford in South London. Her father was the groundsman at a local sports club. Eileen was evacuated in 1939 from Catford to Hastings in East Sussex, and then to Brecon in Wales.

AGNES CONWAY

Agnes was born in 1928 in Howden, near Newcastle upon Tyne. Her father was a teacher in the local Catholic School. Her mother was a teacher too, but had to resign when she got married. Agnes was evacuated to Kendal in 1939.

The government decided to send mothers and children into the countryside to keep them safe. This was known as the evacuation scheme. In this book four people who were young evacuees tell what their lives were like during those troubled times.

ALAN REID

Born in 1934, Alan grew up in Wallington, Surrey. His father worked as an engineer at Wakefields' oil refinery in Surrey Docks in the East End of London. Alan was evacuated from Wallington to Glasgow in 1941, when the German bomber raids on Glasgow had almost finished.

There's a War Coming

In 1939 many children knew their parents were worried. They heard them talk about the German leader, Adolf Hitler. Germany had already invaded Austria and Czechoslovakia. On 1 September, Germany invaded Poland and two days later Britain declared war on Germany.

▲ Adolf Hitler wanted to make Germany the strongest country in Europe. In 1938 his troops marched into Austria and a year later into Czechoslovakia.

EILEEN

I used to listen to the news on the radio and my family discussed what was happening in Europe. My father was a member of the Labour Party and very much against Hitler. We had a Spanish priest helping in the parish. He was a refugee from the Spanish Civil War. He had been bombed and knew how frightening it could be.

On 1 September British evacuation plans rolled into action. More than one and a half million women and children were moved from the cities into the countryside. This was the biggest evacuation of the war, but only the first.

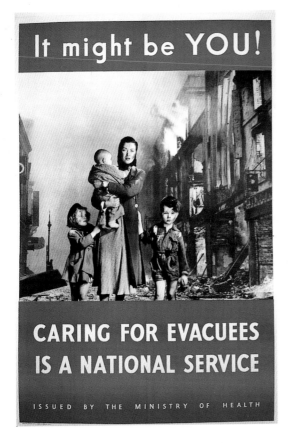

It might be YOU!

CARING FOR EVACUEES IS A NATIONAL SERVICE

ISSUED BY THE MINISTRY OF HEALTH

▲ A pre-war government poster appealing for volunteers to take in evacuees.

By Christmas 1939 many evacuees had returned home because the German bombers had not come. But this peace did not last.

In 1940 and 1941 the Germans launched a series of heavy air raids called the Blitz to bomb the British people to their knees. Three years later, when everyone thought the worst was over, fearsome flying bombs, known as 'doodle-bugs', began to fall in the summer of 1944. Each attack led to mini-evacuations from different cities.

▶ Surrey Docks in the East End of London after a raid.

ALAN

My dad worked in the London docks and he was an air-raid warden there too. They were hit often. It must have been pretty horrific – and for my mother as well – not knowing if he was coming home or not.

Getting Ready to Go

Towns and cities thought to be at risk from bombing were called evacuation areas. Those who wished to go would be moved into safer country areas called reception zones. Sending the children away was hard. There were tears and long hugs as families said goodbye. But there was also a sense of relief for parents, who knew that if their city was bombed, at least their children would be safe.

◀ ▼ Forty million gas masks were issued in 1938. Children had to practise wearing them.

AGNES

I left with my school on Friday 1 September 1939. I took a small case with a change of underwear and pyjamas. I thought we were only going for two weeks. I wasn't too worried because I was going with my friends. I still remember the strong rubbery smell of my gas mask. It was very unpleasant. My father had made a case for my gas mask, but I left it behind. I was so upset – but it was still there in school when I went back in 1943.

JOHN

We were evacuated in 1941 to escape the Glasgow Blitz. I remember being woken in the middle of the night and being carried out by my older brother to the Anderson shelter in the garden. This was covered in earth and had two long benches inside with cushions on. We sat in the dark and listened to the sound of explosions. Luckily our house was not damaged that night but later in the war the windows were blown out.

▲ Many Glasgow children were evacuated in 1941. The city was heavily bombed between March and May and 500 people were killed.

Journey to Safety

During the war few people owned a motor car and even if they did, they probably couldn't use it because petrol was rationed. Nearly all evacuees travelled by train or bus. Many left in school parties organized by local councils and led by their teachers.

EILEEN

London County Council tried to keep family groups together. I went to school at the usual time, bringing my younger brother and two sisters with me. Our cases were already packed and stored at school ready to go. My parents came with us to Greenwich Station and around 10:30 we left on a train to Hastings. I was very emotional but couldn't be too upset in front of my brother and sisters. We stayed together the whole time.

◀ A London school practises for evacuation on 28 August 1939. The children carry their luggage with a change of clothes, a gas mask and food for a day.

Some made their own arrangements, going to stay with relatives or friends instead of strangers. Parents were asked to make sure their children were well equipped with an overcoat, a change of underwear, spare socks, slippers, towel and toothbrush.

We weren't evacuated in 1939 because Wallington was far enough out of London. But in 1941 my mother took me to Glasgow by coach to stay with my two aunts. The journey took around 13 hours in those days because there were no motorways.

AGNES

We travelled in carriages split into compartments of eight. We were a mixture of ages chosen by our teachers, rather than sitting with our friends. I think this was so the older pupils could look after the younger ones. We all took a packed lunch and ate it on the train. I remember that during the journey we stopped at a station and heard the news that Germany had attacked Poland.

▼ A cheerful group of London children wave goodbye as they board the train taking them to the countryside.

Finding New Homes

In reception zones in little towns and villages across the country, billeting officers had collected lists of local families willing to act as foster parents to city children – or to take in adults. If there were not enough volunteers, they could order people to take someone in.

Some evacuees gathered in schools or church halls and waited to be chosen by their hosts. Others were taken in small groups from house to house and either accepted or turned away at the front door.

▲ Evacuees from London arriving in Blackpool. Many people were evacuated to seaside towns because there were plenty of empty hotels and boarding houses normally used by holiday-makers.

EILEEN

When we arrived in Hastings we were taken to an underground car park. We all sat down in little groups and there were crowds and crowds of Hastings residents who had volunteered to take in evacuees. They [the billeting officers] asked… 'Who can take a single child? Who can take a brother and sister?' It was very well organized. Everybody was given a carrier bag with provisions in it. The only thing I can remember is a tin of corned beef.

▲ A group of evacuees arrive at Sherburn from Gateshead and Tynemouth in September 1939.

The government paid foster parents 10 shillings and 6 pence (10s 6d or 52.5p) a week to look after a child aged 10-14; 12s 6d (62.5p) for a 14-16 year old and 15s (75p) for anyone over 16. This money covered food and lodgings. The child's parents had to pay for anything else, like new clothes or school equipment.

JOHN

We were put in an old bothie opposite the big house. That's a tiny old cottage. It had belonged to an estate worker but was terribly damp. After the first night my mother complained and we were moved into the chauffeur's house. This was a small, white, modern bungalow with two bedrooms. It was much better. The chauffeur had to move into a room in the big house, so I don't suppose he was very happy about it.

◄ A billeting officer leaves a large group of children with a foster parent. Taking in five children would be hard work.

Settling In

Evacuation gave the people of Britain a shock. People from different backgrounds were mixed in together – rich and poor, town and country. Children had to learn to live with the families who took them in and many were upset or unhappy. The evacuees in this book were all lucky. They found themselves in good billets and liked their foster parents.

AGNES

I stayed with Mr and Mrs King for a year. They lived in a small terraced house and looking back I think they were quite poor and might have needed the billeting money. [At home] I lived in a modern house, but the Kings' was very different. There was a midden [an outside toilet], that was emptied once a week. There was no bathroom and I had a bath once a week in front of the fire. The water was heated on the range and the cooking – mostly baking and roasting – was done on it too. They looked after me perfectly.

▶ Young evacuees queue up for a bath on a farm in Devon. They are happy – and dirty – after helping in the potato fields for a day.

Many foster parents were appalled at the condition of the young evacuees they looked after. Children from inner city slums often arrived dirty and with only the clothes they stood in. Thousands were poorly fed, infested with lice and carried infectious diseases like scabies.

After a flood of complaints the government acted quickly to improve their health, paying for free milk in schools and cod liver oil for children under five.

'Milk of course, but don't forget Cod Liver Oil & Orange Juice'

▲ A government advert reminds parents about the importance of vitamins for young children. Many poor city children were badly fed.

▲ A matron makes notes on a young patient about to go to the countryside.

ALAN

I had my tonsils out on the table in the dining room. I remember the pad of chloroform being placed over my face. They just put blankets on the table and the operation was carried out by the family doctor. I didn't know what was happening, but it was extremely painful afterwards.

A New Life

As well as learning to live with foster parents, evacuees had to fit into new surroundings. Three of the children in this book went to small country towns, where there was nothing for the Germans to bomb. They had fields and empty lanes to play in instead of bustling streets. They learned how crops were grown and saw wild and farm animals. They ate fresh food and breathed clean air.

HELLO **MUM!**
HELLO **DAD!**

IT'S THE LOVELIEST TIME WE'VE EVER HAD

▲ Postcards like this were sent home by evacuees to let their parents know they were having a good time.

JOHN

The countryside was wonderful for a boy from the city: the fields, animals, woodlands, the river and the 'big house' (where the estate owners lived). We called the river the 'Ohio'. When my big brother wanted us to play by the river he would sing 'Down by the Ohio', the words of a popular song. This was our wartime code so our mother wouldn't know what we were up to.

▶ Boy evacuees helping on a farm. For many city children this was their first trip into the country.

AGNES

In Kendal we weren't far from the Lune Valley. This was full of apple orchards. We used to cycle round and beg for windfalls. One day in September 1941 we were given a day off from school to go and collect blackberries. We took them all back and made blackberry jam. I remember too, there was a river at the bottom of my school grounds with a waterfall. We used to go and watch the salmon jump the waterfall. We never saw anything like that in Newcastle.

▶ Agnes (front left) with her brother and school friends in the ruins of Kendal castle.

EILEEN

Mr Chambers, the father of a friend, ran a coal business. In the summer holidays he would load all the kids – locals and evacuees – on the back of the coal lorry and take us all up to the mountains for picnics. We all clung together and he drove very slowly. There was hardly any traffic. We paddled in the streams, played games. It was just freedom.

War Stories

The war was part of the everyday lives of children from 1939 to 1945. Older brothers, fathers and uncles joined up; food rationing meant a shortage of sweets; the black-out made walking around at night dangerous; bombers droned overhead and air-raid shelters dug in gardens were damp and uncomfortable.

AGNES

We had 4 ozs (125 g) of butter and 4 ozs of margarine per week, kept in little dishes at the side of the dining room, with labels with our names on. I hated margarine and used to swap my 4 oz ration for 2 ozs of butter. When sweets began to disappear we toured the chemists' shops buying Horlicks tablets and chlorodine lozenges, the next best thing.

▲ A week's rations. Rationing meant that everyone had a fair share of food even though there were shortages.

◄ Families with gardens were given Anderson shelters to protect them during air raids. They were covered in soil to deaden the blast from bombs.

Some were taught in strange places such as church halls, libraries or even stately homes and castles. Better still, with books and paper in short supply, lessons became more interesting with nature walks, plays and visits to historic monuments.

AGNES

The teachers at the school did a very good job of keeping us feeling safe and secure. We were taught in the wonderful Sizergh Castle (above), near Kendal. Our lessons took place in the picture gallery with all these paintings on the wall. It was hard to pay attention to the lessons. Our Latin teacher, a nun who was quite a strong character, took us through the North Africa Campaign. That was the time it was going pretty badly! The whole school put on a performance of the *Pirates of Penzance* and everybody was involved. If you weren't singing you were selling programmes.

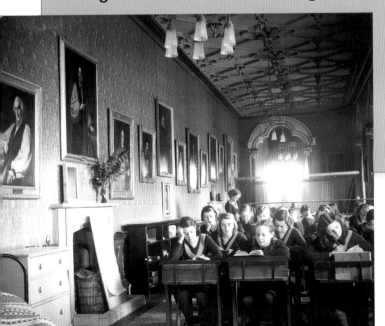

◄ These evacuees are being taught in another grand building, the Bishop of Chichester's Palace in West Sussex.

23

Home Visits and Dangers

Visits by busy parents, who might live hundreds of miles away, were all too rare. But evacuees sometimes went home for their 'holidays'. This meant leaving the safety of the country and taking a chance in the towns. After months apart, families could seem like strangers.

EILEEN

We didn't see our parents very often. We missed them all the time. We got letters every week with postal orders for our pocket money and birthday presents. During Christmas 1940 the local people in Brecon invited all the parents from London to come and stay – so it was still like a family Christmas. It must have been a tremendous effort for them.

Off to Rejoin School

("Evening Chronicle" Photo.)
ALL WITH SMILING FACES. Pupils of St. Cuthbert's Grammar School, Newcastle, pictured as they left the Central Station, Newcastle, to-day, for Cockermouth, where they will rejoin their school after holidays at home.

▲ Children like Agnes were evacuated from many Newcastle schools to the Lake District and came home for holidays.

AGNES

When I was at home for Easter 1941 the house was hit by the blast from a landmine exploding in the next street. The windows blew out and the ceilings came down. We were on our way to the garden shelter when three more landmines fell. My father was an air-raid warden getting ready to go out and he was blown over by the blast. I think about eight people were killed.

▲ Agnes's home in Howden, North Tyneside before it was bombed.

CHILDREN RETURN TO RECEPTION AREA

Pupils from the Convent of the Sacred Heart, Fenham, Newcastle, to-day returned to Kendal after having spent a happy Christmas holiday at home. They were given a cheery send-off by their parents at Newcastle Central Station. There were no tears . . . only smiles. Some of the younger children carried their favourite Christmas toys. There were about 100 children on the train.

▲ Agnes's school returns to the Lake District after coming home for Christmas 1939.

ALAN

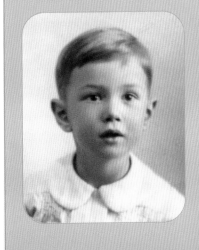

I soon picked up a Scottish accent and when I went home I could hardly remember my mother. She was Scottish but I thought she sounded very English.

Back Home

Our evacuees were all home by 1943 and spent the rest of the war with their families. Everyone thought the worst of the bombing was over, but in June 1944 the Germans launched their V1 flying bombs. Over 2,000 exploded in London and 6,184 civilians were killed.

◀ This photograph shows the damage caused to a food store by a flying bomb at Wandsworth in London. The rescue workers are clearing wreckage and saving scarce tins of corned beef.

EILEEN

The whole school went back to London at the end of the summer holidays in August 1943. We went on a train, like evacuation in reverse, to Paddington Station and my parents were there to meet us. In the meantime my Mum and Dad had been bombed out of our home and we rented the house next door. We lived in what was known as 'Cemetery Lane' because so many people had been killed. Four doors up from us there were just gaps.... My mother was injured in a daylight raid.

ALAN

Rationing seemed bad in London. It was a struggle for my mother. We ate everything on our plates, except cabbage….

We saw the doodle-bugs – they looked very small. I watched one dive. I was kneeling down to get a good sight of it and felt the blast, even though I was a long way off. It made a funny sound: put, put, put – like a lawn mower engine.

The dangers and hardships lasted until VE Day, on 8 May 1945, which brought an end to the fighting in Europe.

▼ After six long and hard years of war, Britain celebrated VE (Victory in Europe) day with thousands of street parties.

Staying in Touch

Evacuation was a huge adventure. The children were away from home for months or even years and grew up quickly. They became self-sufficient and adaptable.

Throughout the war a total of 3.5 million children were evacuated. They lived through one of the most remarkable episodes in British history, sharing funny and sad experiences and often making friends for life.

AGNES

Mrs King [foster parent in Kendal] died not long after the war. We stayed in touch with Mr King; in fact he came here a couple of times for a holiday…. I'm going to an old girls' lunch next week and 99 per cent of the people who will be there were in my evacuation group.

ALAN

I stayed very close to both my aunts after the war. Neither of them had children of their own, so it was as if my brother and I had three families. We saw them several times a year until they died.

Many stayed in touch with their foster parents for years. Societies like the Evacuees Reunion Association help former evacuees stay in touch with each other.

EVACUEES REUNION ASSOCIATION
ANNIVERSARY OF THE
EVACUATION 1939-1999

In Association with NPI
ESTABLISHED IN 1835

▲ The Evacuees Reunion Association was founded in 1996 to help former evacuees keep in touch and talk about their experiences. They also operate an education service for schools.

EILEEN

I met my first boyfriend, Jeff, in Brecon in 1940 when I was 14. We were just friends and had the odd kiss and cuddle. We kept in touch… and believe it or not he came to stay with me last summer.

JOHN

We didn't become friends with the owners of the big house and didn't stay in touch after the war. They were too grand. But I did go back years later for a look. I was surprised at how small everything seemed – like the chauffeur's bungalow – compared to my childhood memories.

▲ Many schools today teach about the evacuation and children like these make labels and gas masks to use in mock evacuations.

Glossary

Air-raid sirens sirens situated throughout the towns on buildings like schools to warn people of air attacks by enemy planes.

Air-raid wardens officers who helped people during air raids.

Anderson shelter air-raid shelter made from corrugated iron covered with earth.

Billeting officers officials in charge of finding accommodation for the evacuees.

Billets accommodation.

Black-out making sure no lights showed so that enemy bombers had a harder time finding targets.

Blitz a heavy air raid.

Boiler-maker person who made boilers for steam engines.

Chauffeur driver.

Chlorodine lozenges cough sweets.

Copper plate handwriting best joined up handwriting.

Corned beef beef preserved in salt and tinned.

Evacuation zones places most likely to be bombed.

Evacuee a person who has been evacuated from their home.

Foster parents people who had young evacuees to stay.

Groundsman person in charge of keeping the sports pitches in good order.

Honeymoon suite a smart room for a newly married couple.

Horlicks tablets tablets that taste like a Horlicks drink.

Join up join one of the armed services – Army, Navy or Air Force.

Labour Party the political party that supported the rights of ordinary working people.

Landmine a huge bomb that was dropped on the end of a parachute.

Midden a toilet that needed to be emptied every week. It was not connected to drains like a flush toilet.

North Africa Campaign the war in the deserts of Egypt and Libya against German and Italian troops.

Parish the area in which a church is situated and the people who attend the Church.

Pirates of Penzance a light opera by the famous Victorian composers Gilbert and Sullivan.

Postal orders cheques that could only be bought and cashed at a post office. This was safer than sending cash in envelopes.

Poverty being poor.

Provisions food and supplies.

Quarantined when a person with an infectious disease is kept separate from other people.

RADAR short for Radio Detection And Ranging. A way of detecting planes in the air by bouncing radio waves off them.

Range a large fire, oven and water heater built into the chimney of a house.

Rear gunner gunner at the back of a plane.

Reception zones areas accepting those who had been evacuated.

Rote learning by constant repetition of a fact.

Scabies a disease that spreads easily and causes itchy skin.

Slums areas of poor housing.

Spanish Civil War war in Spain between the Nationalists (backed by Germany) and Republicans (backed by Russia).

VE Day Victory in Europe Day.

Voluntary not forced on people.

Further Reading

Non-fiction

Ingliss, Ruth, *The Children's War*, Collins, 1989.

Parsons, Martin, *Waiting to Go Home: Letters and Reminiscences from the Evacuation*, DSM Technical Publications, 1999.

Reynoldson, Fiona, *The Home Front: Evacuation*, Hodder Wayland, 1990.

Ross, Stewart, *The Home Front*, Wayland, 1990.

Westall, Robert, *Children of the Blitz*, Macmillan, 1999.

Fiction

Crompton, Richmal, *William and the Evacuees*, Macmillan Children's Books, 1987.

Resources

Places to Visit

The Imperial War Museum in London is the best place to find out what life was like during the Second World War.

You could also visit 'Imperial War Museum North', in Trafford Wharf Road, Manchester.

Index

Numbers in *italics* indicate photographs.